ORIGAMI
Magic

17 amazing tricks, puzzles and illusions

STEVE BIDDLE

Illustrations by
MEGUMI BIDDLE

CONNECTIONS
BOOK PUBLISHING

To John Fisher, Peter Lane, Graham Reed and Chris Woodward,
heroes of magic.

A CONNECTIONS EDITION
This edition published in Great Britain in 2012 by
Connections Book Publishing Limited
St Chad's House, 148 King's Cross Road, London WC1X 9DH
www.connections-publishing.com

British Library Cataloguing-in-Publication data available on request.

ISBN 978-1-85906-339-2

10 9 8 7 6 5 4 3 2 1

Phototypeset in Amazone BT, Stone and Folio BT
using InDesign on Apple Macintosh
Printed in China

Contents

Introduction

Welcome to the amazing world of origami magic – a world where the impossible is made to appear possible. Discover how, with just a few sheets of paper and one or two other everyday materials found around the home (or available from any good stationery store), you can create the kind of magic that will entertain, astound and truly bewilder your family and friends. This exciting book is packed with paper folds to create mystifying puzzles, amazing tricks and fantastic illusions. With wonders like these, you can enter the realms of magic.

The development of paper folding in the West can be traced back to a company of Japanese jugglers who visited Europe in the 1860s. The jugglers brought with them the method for folding a 'flapping bird', and soon directions on how to make this – along with other puzzling folds – were appearing in various European publications. Later, many famous magicians, including David Devant, Harry Houdini, Cy Endfield and Robert Harbin, became especially interested in paper folding, attesting to the link between origami and magic, which still continues to this today.

The origami projects
The projects in the book are divided into four groups:

• **Amazing tricks** Prepare to be astonished as all kinds of things are made to happen from just a single sheet of paper. That in itself is quite a trick!
• **Perplexing puzzles** Make paper replicas of traditional puzzles that will tease, baffle and delight anyone who tries to solve them.
• **Impossible illusions** Discover paper illusions that appear to defy belief and will keep your audience guessing!
• **Crafty cuts, tears and folds** Learn traditional cutting, tearing and folding techniques that have been impressing audiences for years.

With origami magic, presentation is key. Simply knowing the secret of a trick or puzzle won't make you a good magician – you need to try it out in private, several times, before attempting your performance. Practise the moves until you can perform a trick sufficiently well without looking at your hands and disclosing its secret. Look at your audience with a warm smile on your face and make them believe, through your movements, words and appearance, that you are truly an entertainer!

If dinner guests ask you to show them an origami trick, be prepared. Keep a few sheets of paper or a newspaper to hand (always use the classified or financial pages, so that there are no areas of bold print to spoil the symmetry of the finished design), and then you'll be ready to perform at any time.

Putting on a perfomance

If you decide to put on a proper show with the projects in the book, your performance should include:

- a very good – and unexpected – opening
- a few entertaining tricks in the middle to keep up the audience's interest
- an exceptionally good trick to end with

Always try to build a story around each item that you present – something engaging, entertaining, and suited to your personality. Try to limit your show to no more than five tricks at the most, so that your audience remains enrapt and not bored! And never disclose how a trick or puzzle is accomplished; keep their secrets to yourself. Above all, respect your magic when performing; if you don't, then neither will your audience.

Don't worry if a trick goes wrong – it happens to all of us at sometime. You'll find that, with experience, you will learn to cover up your mistake, and the chances are that your audience will never spot the error.

Paper folding already has a certain magic about it. The very fact that a model so complex (or delightfully simple) can be created from just a piece of paper is magic in itself. People assume it can't be done; the paper-folder, like the magician, performs the inconceivable – sometimes with surprising results. When the 'flapping bird' flutters its wings between your fingertips, or the origami 'rabbit' magically appears, and you have put on an extremely good show, you will hopefully be rewarded with the most wonderful sound that any entertainer aims to receive: applause!

Steve Biddle

Helpful tips

Before you begin any of the projects in this book, read through the following tips designed to make origami easier.

- Before you start, make sure your paper is the correct shape.

- Do your folding on a smooth, flat surface such as a table or large book. Ensure that your folds are neat and accurate.

- Press your folds into place with your thumbnail.

- In the diagrams in this book, the shading represents the coloured side of the paper.

- Look at each diagram carefully, read the instructions, then look at the next diagram to see what shape should be created once you have completed the step you are working on.

- You will find it easiest to work your way through from the beginning of the book to the end, as some of the projects and procedures in later sections are based partially on previous ones. However, if you are an experienced paper-folder and can follow origami instructions without too much help, feel free to select any design as a starting point.

- Many of the models can be folded from one square or rectangle of paper, but some require more. The instructions at the start of each project clearly state what you will need. If you are using your own paper rather than the paper supplied with this book, make sure it is cut absolutely square. There is nothing more frustrating that trying to fold a nearly square square!

- If a fold or whole model doesn't work out, don't give up hope. Go through the illustrations one by one, checking that you have read the instructions correctly. If you are still unable to complete the model, put it to one side and come back to it later with a fresh mind.

- Always take care when using cutting tools or sharp implements (youngsters should ask for help from an adult when making any projects requiring the use of scissors, a craft knife or a needle and cotton). When using a craft knife be sure to cut on a piece of old board or on a cutting mat, so that you don't cut yourself or damage any surfaces.

Symbols and the basics of folding

The symbols that form the basis of the instructions in this book are used internationally. They show the direction in which the paper should be folded. If you are new to origami, I suggest that you take a few squares of paper and study the following symbols and folding procedures before trying any of the origami projects. Look at the diagrams carefully to see which way the dashes, dots and arrows go over, through and under the paper, and fold your paper accordingly.

1 Valley fold

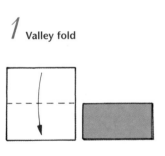

A valley fold (fold towards you or in front) is shown by a line of dashes and a solid arrow showing the direction in which the paper has to be folded.

2 Mountain fold

A mountain fold (fold away from you or behind) is shown by a line of dots and dashes and a hollow-headed arrow. As in the valley fold, the arrow shows the direction in which the paper has to be folded.

3 Fold and unfold

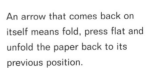

An arrow that comes back on itself means fold, press flat and unfold the paper back to its previous position.

4 Step fold

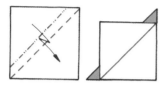

A zigzagged arrow drawn on top of the diagram means fold the paper in the direction shown by the arrow. A step fold is made by pleating the paper in a valley and mountain fold.

5 Fold over and over

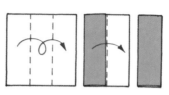

A looped arrow drawn on top of a diagram means keep folding the paper over in the direction shown by the arrow. Each fold-line represents one fold-over move.

6 Outside reverse fold

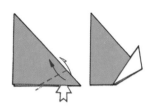

Solid and hollow-headed arrows and valley and mountain fold-lines instruct you to separate the layers of paper, taking one to the front and one to the back.

10 Turn around

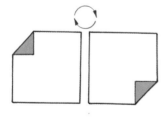

Two circling arrows means turn the paper (or model) around into the position shown.

11 Cut

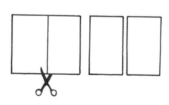

A pair of scissors and a solid line means cut the paper. The solid line shows the position of the cut.

12 Insert

An arrow with the tail broken near the head means insert the flap or point either into a pocket or underneath a layer of paper.

7 Inside reverse fold

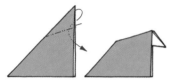

A wavy arrow with a broken tail
and a mountain fold-line means
pull the point inside the model,
in the direction indicated by the
wavy arrow.

8 Open and squash

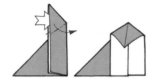

A hollow arrow with a short,
indented tail instructs you to
open out the layers of paper
and squash them down neatly
into the position shown in the
following diagram.

9 Turn over

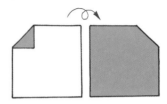

A looped arrow means turn the
paper (or model) over in the
direction shown.

13 Enlarge

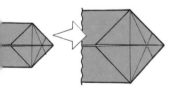

A swollen arrow with a pointed
tail means that the following
diagram is drawn to a larger scale.
To clarify a tricky (or detailed)
procedure, an enlargement of it
is illustrated inside a circle.

14 Roll up

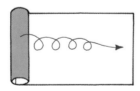

An arrow with a series of loops
in its tail drawn on top of the
diagram means roll the paper up
in the direction shown by the
arrow.

How to make A-sized paper

Currently, there is one widespread international standard paper size (ISO) and a localized standard used in North America.

Some of the projects in this book require rectangular paper, and can be made with either A4 (210 x 297 mm) or letter (8.5 x 11 in) paper, and A3 (297 x 420 mm) or ledger (11 x 17 in) paper, as specified. The Pyramid (page 27), however, can only be made using A-sized paper, as the width-to-height ratio of the rectangle is key. So, if A-sized paper is not readily available where you live (or you simply don't have any to hand), here is a quick and easy method for making an A-sized rectangle from *any* paper size.

Use a rectangle of paper. You will also need a pair of scissors.

1

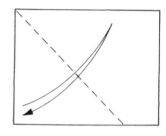

Turn the rectangle of paper sideways on. Valley fold the left-hand side up to meet the top edge. Press flat and unfold it.

5

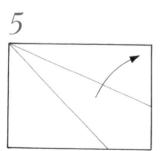

... an A-sized rectangle.

6

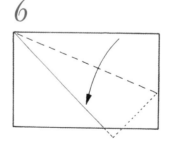

If, in step 2, the top right-hand corner protrudes beyond the bottom edge ...

7

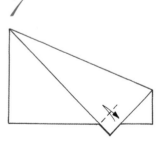

... valley fold the protruding corner up to where the sloping and bottom edges intersect. Press the paper only a little, as shown. Unfold it.

2

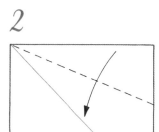

Valley fold the top edge down to lie against the diagonal fold-line (if the top-right corner protrudes beyond the bottom edge, go to step 6).

3

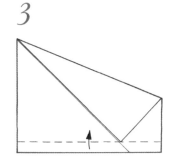

Valley fold the bottom edge up along a horizontal line as shown. Press flat and unfold it.

4

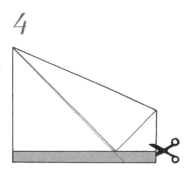

Carefully cut along the fold-line made in step 3 and discard the shaded strip of paper. To complete, open out the paper into ...

8

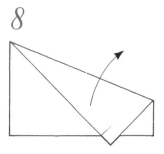

Open out the paper.

9

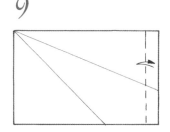

Valley fold the right-hand side over along a vertical line, following the fold mark you made in step 7, as shown. Press flat and unfold it.

10

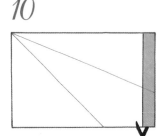

Carefully cut along the fold-line made in step 9 and discard the shaded strip of paper to produce an A-sized rectangle.

Tumbler

This delightful, simple action toy is based on a model originally created by the late Seiryo Takekawa. Why not try a game of tumbler toppling? Fold a few tumblers and stand them upright in a line, an equal distance apart. Then topple the first one, which knocks the second one over, which topples onto the third … continuing until all the tumblers have fallen, with a 'rat-tat-tat'!

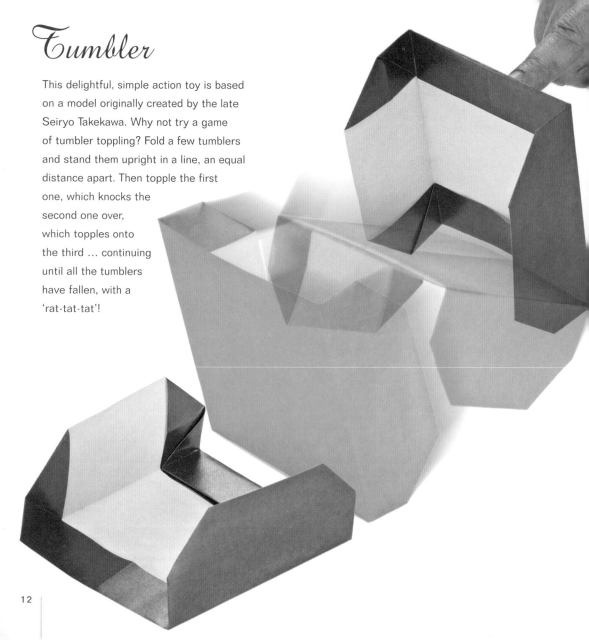

Making your tumbler

Use one piece of A4 or letter paper, white side up.

1

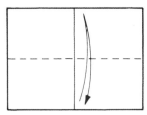

Turn the rectangle of paper sideways on. Fold and unfold it in half from side to side.

2

Fold and unfold in half from bottom to top.

3

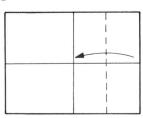

Valley fold the right-hand side into the middle, making a flap of paper.

4

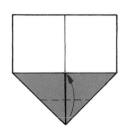

Turn the paper around, so that the flap is at the bottom. Valley fold the flap's bottom corners up to meet the vertical middle fold-line, making a shape that looks like an upside-down roof.

5

Valley fold the bottom point up to meet the roof's horizontal edges.

6

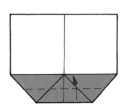

Valley fold the new bottom edge up …

7

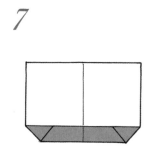

... to meet the roof's horizontal edges. Press the paper flat.

8

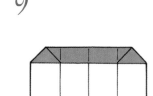

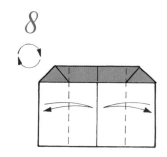

Turn the paper around into the position shown. Valley fold the sides into the middle. Press flat and unfold them.

9

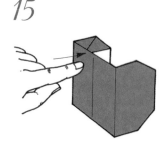

Valley fold the bottom corners up to meet their adjacent vertical fold-lines, making two triangles.

13

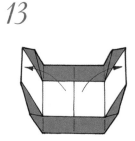

To complete the tumbler, unfold the doors, so that they stand upright.

14

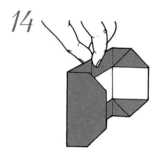

Stand the tumbler on a flat surface, with its doors facing away from you and the thickest part of the model at the top.

15

Gently push its top edge with your finger as shown, and this puzzling piece of origami will ...

10

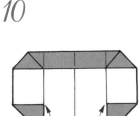

Valley fold the bottom edge up to lie along the top edges of the two triangles.

11

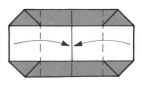

Once again, valley fold the sides into the middle, making ...

12

... two doors. Press the paper flat.

16

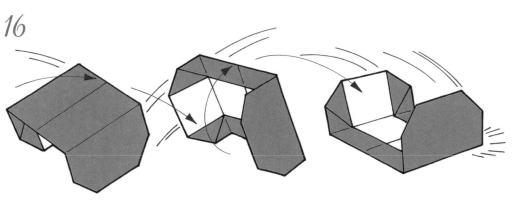

... roll forwards, turning a somersault with a 'rat-tat-tat'!

Monkey climbing Mount Fuji

Also known among paper-folders as 'chicken laying a square egg' or 'crawling beetle', this captivating Japanese action model has an unusual finale that may take unprepared observers by surprise!

Making your monkey climbing Mount Fuji

The starting point for this paper fold begins with the preliminary fold, so called because it is the foundation for several origami bases. Use a square piece of paper, white side up. You will also need a pair of scissors.

1

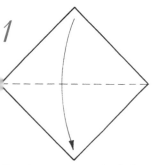

Turn the square around to look like a diamond. Valley fold it in half from top to bottom, making a diaper fold.

2

Valley fold the diaper fold in half from right to left.

3

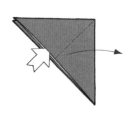

Lift up the left-hand side of the top layer. Open the paper and …

4

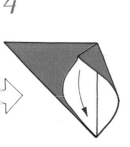

… squash it down neatly …

5

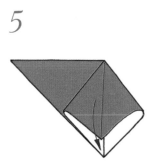

… into a diamond.

6

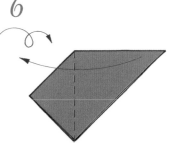

Turn the paper over. Valley fold the right-hand triangular flap over to the left, as though turning the page of a book.

17

7

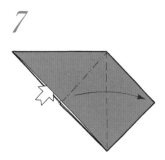

Repeat steps 3 to 5, making a preliminary fold.

8

Fold and unfold the front flap of paper in half from bottom to top.

9

Valley fold the flap's tip into the middle.

13

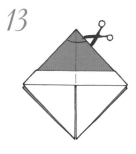

Carefully cut off (or simply tear off) the preliminary fold's tip in a cone-like shape, as shown, making the monkey. The remaining part of the model represents Mount Fuji.

14

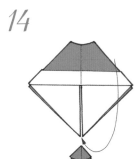

Slip the monkey onto Mount Fuji's lower points. The points ...

15

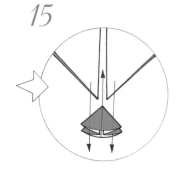

... should go between the monkey's front and back flaps of paper, adjacent to the middle line.

10

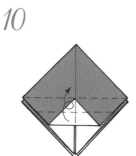

Valley fold the folded edge up to the middle and …

11

… then over along the middle. Press the paper flat.

12

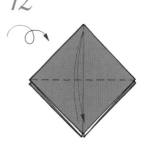

Turn the paper over. Repeat steps 9 to 11 with the front flap of paper.

16

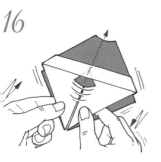

Between the thumb and forefinger of each hand, hold Mount Fuji's lower points as shown. Agitate the points by moving each hand back and forth quickly, and you'll find that the monkey will start to climb upwards.

17

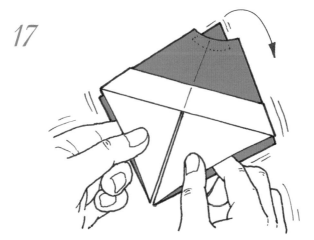

Keep on agitating the points and the monkey's route will take it up inside Mount Fuji. Watch the conically shaped hole at the top until you see the monkey appear and finally drop through.

Magic tipper

The magic tipper is brought to life by
two internal triangular flaps that push
against each other. Watch it slowly lift
its tail – and then suddenly tip up, as
if by magic. If the model tips over
too quickly, or fails to tip at all,
the flaps may need adjusting.

Making your magic tipper

Take care when making your magic tipper: as you construct it the layers will accumulate, meaning that the paper will tear easily. Use a square piece of paper, white side up.

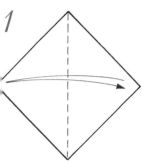

1

Turn the square around to look like a diamond. Fold and unfold it in half from side to side.

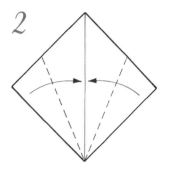

2

From the bottom point, valley fold the lower sloping edges into the middle, making a kite base.

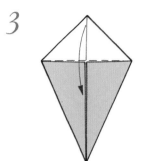

3

Valley fold the kite base's top point down over the horizontal edges.

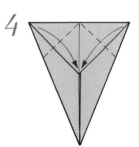

4

Valley fold the top corners down to lie either side of the middle fold-line. The model will become very thick, so a certain amount of space must be left in the middle to facilitate step 7 later on.

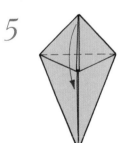

5

Valley fold the top point down on a line between the two side points.

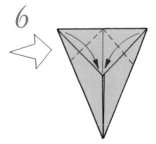

6

Valley fold the top corners down to lie either side of the middle fold-line.

7

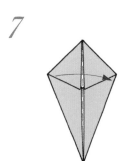

Valley fold in half from left to right, taking great care at this stage that the paper does not tear.

8

The magic tipper is now complete.

9

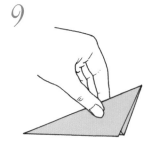

Place the magic tipper on a clean flat surface in the position shown. It should gradually …

10

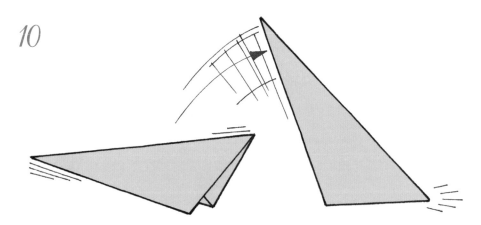

… lift its tail and then tip up suddenly! The speed of the tip is determined by the strength of the folds made in step 6. The harder the folds, the slower the tip. Ideally, the tip should be as slow as possible.

Flapping bird

This charming paper fold is guaranteed to
bring a smile to anyone's face once they
discover the secret to making the wings flap.

Making your flapping bird

$\mathcal{U}$se a square piece of paper, white side up.

1

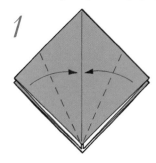

Follow steps 1 to 7 of the monkey climbing Mount Fuji (see page 17) to make a preliminary fold. From the bottom point, valley fold the lower (open) sloping edges into the middle.

2

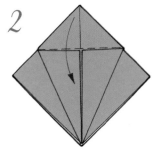

The top layer of paper should now look like an ice cream cone, with a triangle of ice cream at the top and the cone below. Valley fold the 'ice cream' down and over the cone.

3

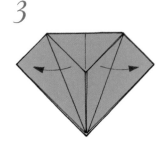

Unfold the edges from underneath the 'ice cream', as if opening the doors of a cupboard.

7

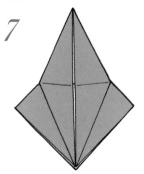

Press the paper flat, making it diamond-shaped. This completes the petal fold.

8

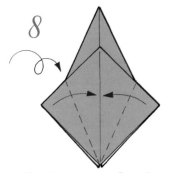

Turn the paper over. From the bottom point, valley fold the lower (open) sloping edges into the middle. Repeat steps 2 to 7 ...

9

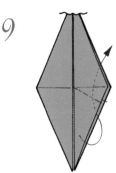

... making a bird base. Make the bird's neck by inside reverse folding the bottom right-hand point as follows:

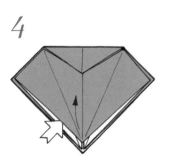

4

Now make a petal fold. This is
what you do: pinch and lift up
the front flap of paper.

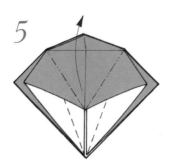

5

Continue to lift up the flap,
making …

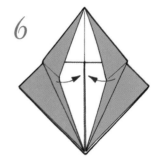

6

… its edges meet in the middle.

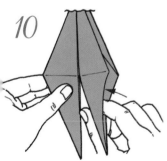

10

Place your forefinger into the
point's groove and, with your
thumb underneath …

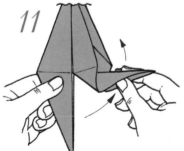

11

… push the point up inside
itself …

12

… into the position shown. To
complete, press the paper flat.

13

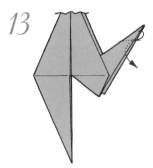

Inside reverse fold the neck's tip to make the beak.

14

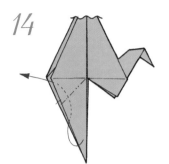

Make the bird's tail by inside reverse folding the bottom left-hand point into the position shown in step 15.

15

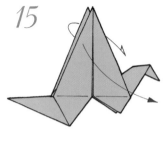

Give the wings a gentle curve, so completing the flapping bird.

16

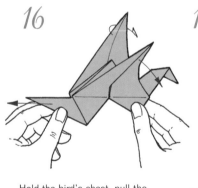

Hold the bird's chest, pull the tail and ...

17

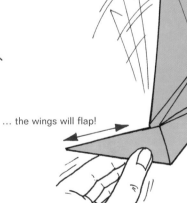

... the wings will flap!

Pyramid

Step into the shoes of an Ancient Egyptian and face your own construction challenge: can you assemble the four identical pieces into a pyramid? It's a great puzzle to leave on a desk or coffee table for people to try, as it looks easier than it is …

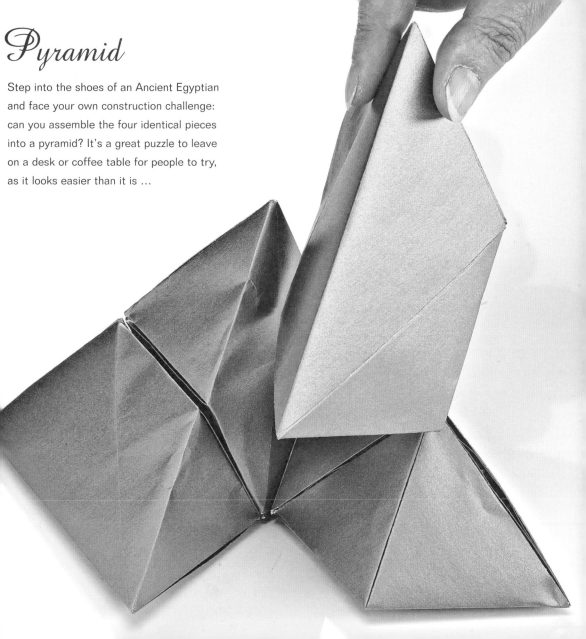

Making your pyramid

The pyramid is known as an assembly puzzle, in which identical pieces are arranged in a certain way to form a particular shape. Use four pieces of A4 paper, white side up.

1

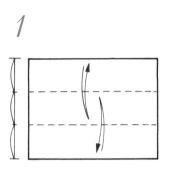

Take one piece of paper and turn it sideways on. Divide it horizontally into three equal sections by valley folding, then open up again.

2

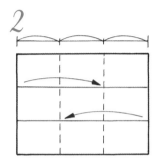

Valley fold the right-hand side over to a point one-third of the way from the left. Valley fold the left-hand side over so that it lies on top.

3

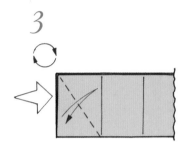

Turn the paper around into the position shown. Valley fold the left-hand panel in half along one diagonal as shown. Press flat and unfold it.

7

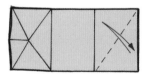

Repeat steps 3 to 6 with the right-hand panel.

8

Turn the paper over. Fold and unfold the middle panel in half along a diagonal line from top right to bottom left.

9

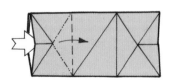

Stand the left-hand panel upright along the adjacent vertical fold-line. Using the existing fold-lines, open out the panel, taking …

4

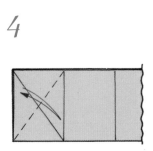

Valley fold the left-hand panel in half along its other diagonal. Press flat and unfold it.

5

Valley fold the left-hand side of the left-hand panel in half from bottom to top, being careful ...

6

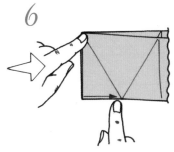

... only to press on the paper from the panel's side to its middle point. Unfold it.

10

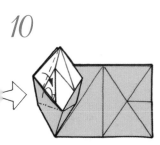

... one layer of paper to one side and two to the other as shown. Along the sloping fold-lines, push the two-layered side inwards.

11

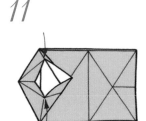

Bring the top and bottom points together, making the panel become three-dimensional, while at the same time ...

12

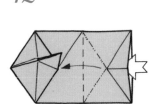

... producing a triangular flap. Repeat steps 9 to 11 with the right-hand panel.

13

Position the triangular flaps so that the left-hand one points downwards and the right-hand one points upwards. Refold the middle panel's existing diagonal fold-line, while at the same time …

14

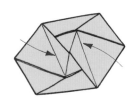

… inserting the triangular flaps deep under the opposite sloping sides as shown.

15

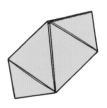

Firm up the folds, so completing one piece of the pyramid.

16

Repeat steps 1 to 15 with the remaining three pieces of paper. Turn the pieces around and place them together as shown to …

17

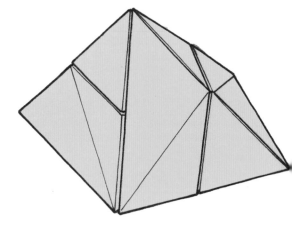

… build the pyramid. This is not difficult – nor is it as easy as you may think!

Tangram

This popular Chinese dissection puzzle consists of seven flat geometrical pieces, called 'tans', which are put together to form an infinite variety of recognizable shapes. The challenge is to create specific shapes (given only an outline) using all seven pieces, without any pieces overlapping. Sounds simple? Give it a try ...

Making your tangram

*T*o make the seven pieces, you will need four squares of paper, identical in size, white side up. You will also need a pair of scissors and pencil.

1

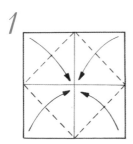

Two large triangles: Fold and unfold one square in half from bottom to top and side to side. Then valley fold the corners into the middle, making a blintz base.

2

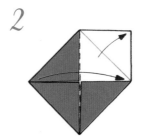

Unfold the blintz base's top right-hand corner and then valley fold in half from left to right.

3

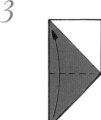

Valley fold in half from bottom to top.

7

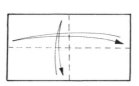

Parallelogram: Turn rectangle C sideways on, with the white side on top. Fold and unfold it in half from bottom to top and side to side.

8

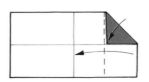

Valley fold the top right-hand corner down to meet the adjacent horizontal fold-line and then valley fold the right-hand side into the middle.

9

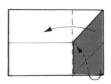

Inside reverse fold the bottom right-hand corner and then, along the adjacent vertical fold-line, valley fold the right-hand side over to the left.

4

Insert the top right-hand corner into the adjacent sloping pocket, so completing one large triangle.

5

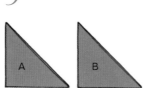

Repeat steps 1 to 4 with another square. Label the triangles A and B.

6

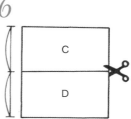

Fold and unfold another square in half from bottom to top. Carefully cut along the middle fold-line, making rectangles C and D.

10

Inside reverse fold the top right-hand corner and then valley fold the top left-hand corner down to meet the adjacent horizontal fold-line.

11

Valley fold in half from left to right, while at the same time inserting the left-hand side underneath the right-hand layers of paper.

12

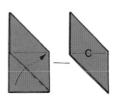

Insert the lower left-hand corner into the adjacent sloping pocket, so completing the parallelogram. Label the parallelogram C.

13

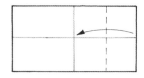

Square: Repeat step 7 with rectangle D. Valley fold the right-hand side into the middle.

14

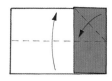

Valley fold the top right-hand corner down to meet the adjacent horizontal fold-line and then valley fold in half from bottom to top.

15

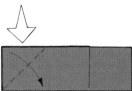

Valley fold the left-hand side down to lie along the bottom edge, making a triangular point.

19

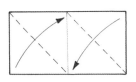

Medium-sized triangle: Turn rectangle E sideways on, with the white side on top. Valley fold the right-hand side down to lie along the bottom edge and valley fold the left-hand side up to lie along the top edge.

20

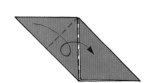

Valley fold the top left-hand point down to meet the bottom edge and then, along the adjacent vertical fold-line, valley fold it over to the right.

21

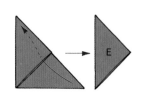

Insert the bottom right-hand point into the adjacent sloping pocket, so completing the medium-sized triangle. Label the triangle E.

16

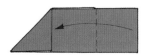

Valley fold the right-hand side over to meet the triangle's vertical edge.

17

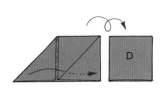

Valley fold in half from left to right, while at the same time inserting the triangular point into the adjacent sloping pocket. Turn the paper over, so completing the square. Label the square D.

18

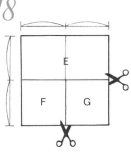

Fold and unfold the remaining square in half from bottom to top and side to side. Carefully cut along the middle fold-lines, making rectangle E and squares F and G.

22

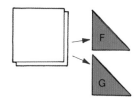

Two small triangles: Repeat steps 1 to 4 with squares F and G, so completing the two small triangles. Label the triangles F and G.

23

This is the completed tangram square. Shuffle the seven pieces and then try to rearrange them into a square without looking at the illustration. Have some fun creating different shapes – see if your audience can guess what they are.

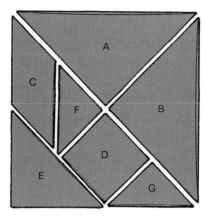

Flexi-cube

This modular-origami puzzle
(where simple shapes or units
are fitted together to build more
complex constructions) can be twisted in a
continuous loop-like motion to reveal pattern ...
after pattern ... after pattern. Once the basic cube has
been mastered, it is an easy item to use as a construction
piece when making solid geometrical shapes.

Making your flexi-cube

*T*ry making the cubes in several different colours. Use forty-eight squares of paper (six for each cube), identical in size, coloured side up. You will also need a roll of clear sticky tape.

1

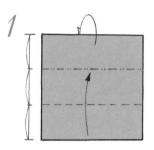

Making a cube: Valley fold the bottom edge of one square over to a point one-third of the way to the top. Then mountain fold the top edge behind to meet the bottom.

2

Valley fold the right-hand side up to lie along the top edge and valley fold the left-hand side down to lie along the bottom edge, making triangular points.

3

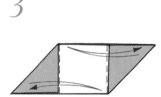

Along their adjacent vertical edges, valley fold the right- and left-hand triangular points over the centre square. Press flat and unfold them, completing one unit.

4

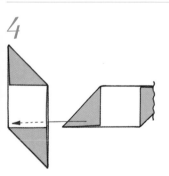

Repeat steps 1 to 3 with another five squares. Take two units and join them together by inserting the triangular point of one into the side pocket of another as shown.

5

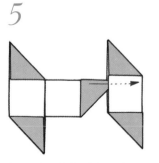

Insert the third unit into place. You are now halfway there!

6

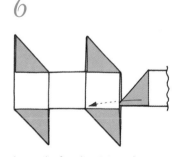

Insert the fourth unit into place. This one is easy.

7

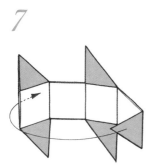

To join the units, carefully insert the right-hand triangular point into the left-hand side pocket. The cube will now begin to take shape.

8

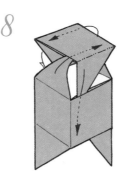

From the top, insert the fifth unit into place by inserting the triangular points into side pockets as shown.

9

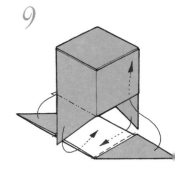

From the bottom, repeat step 8 with the sixth unit.

13

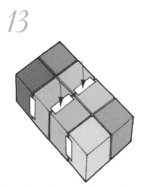

Join the cubes together in the middle with sticky tape as shown.

14

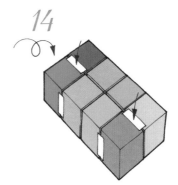

Carefully turn the cubes over. Join the cubes together at the ends with sticky tape as shown, so completing the flexi-cube.

15

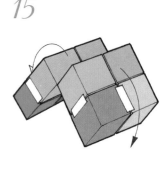

The flexi-cube can be folded (flexed) over many times in a continuous loop-like action until it disintegrates between your fingers.

10

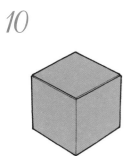

Firm up the units, so completing the cube. Repeat steps 1 to 10 with the remaining forty-two squares of paper, making a further seven cubes.

11

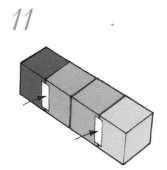

Making the flexi-cube: Lay four cubes side by side and join them together along the side with sticky tape as shown. Repeat with the remaining four cubes.

12

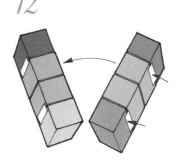

Lay the cubes side by side in two rows of four, with the sticky tape on the outside.

16

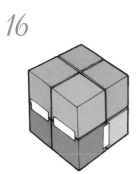

Flex it inside out, and ...

17

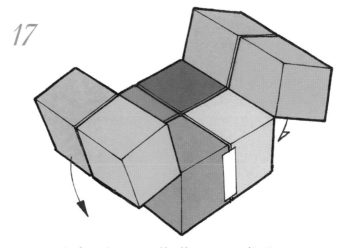

... over again, for as long as you like. How many combinations can you find?

Inside-out puzzle

The concept of this puzzling piece of origami is based on a mathematical curiosity known as a flexagon – a folded-paper construction that can be flexed along its folds to reveal and conceal its faces alternately. Here, the trick is to make a paper box and turn it inside out with just a few folds, without cutting or tearing the paper in any way.

Making your inside-out puzzle

$\mathcal{U}$se a rectangle of paper, 4 x 1 in proportion, white side up (use strong, stiff paper that will easily bend when folded back and forth a few times). You will also need a roll of clear sticky tape.

1

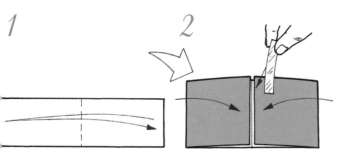

Turn the rectangle of paper sideways on. Fold and unfold it in half from side to side.

2

Valley fold the sides into the middle and join the vertical edges together with sticky tape, making a box without a top or bottom.

3

Valley fold the box's opposite corners together in turn to mark the diagonal fold-lines as shown. Press flat and unfold them.

4

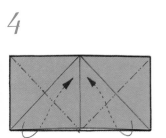

So how do you turn the box inside out without disfiguring the paper in any way? Along the diagonal fold-lines made in step 3, inside reverse fold the box's two bottom corners, making a triangle.

5

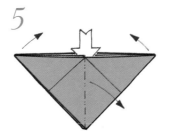

Hold the triangle's top edges in either hand and pull them apart, collapsing it …

6

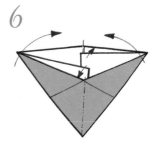

… down into a diamond, while making sure that the two inside flaps go in opposite directions, one forwards and the other backwards, as shown. Press the paper flat.

7

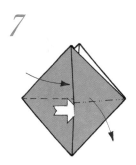

Open out the diamond's right-hand pocket of paper, pulling it ...

8

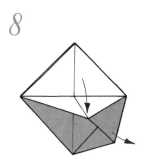

... over towards the right, while at the same time valley folding its top point down ...

9

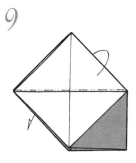

... to meet the bottom point. Repeat steps 7 to 9 behind, making a tube.

13

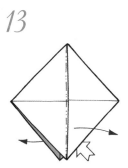

Hold the diamond's bottom points in either hand and pull them apart, collapsing it ...

14

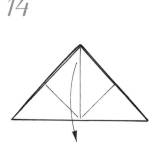

... down into a triangle. Fold the triangle's front flap of paper down.

15

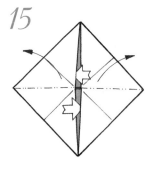

Place your fingers underneath the paper's vertical middle edges and gently pull your hands apart. The paper will open out into a box-like shape (with no top or bottom) and you will discover ...

10

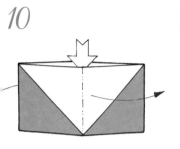

Hold the tube's top edges in either hand and pull them apart, taking its front layer across to the right and its back layer to the left.

11

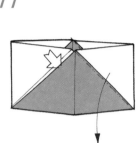

Insert your forefinger between the left-hand layers of paper and pull the top layer downwards, while at the same time ...

12

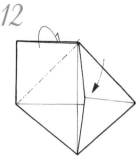

... bringing the top right-hand edges over to lie along the vertical middle line. Repeat steps 11 and 12 behind, making a diamond.

16

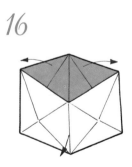

... that the puzzle will now be inside out!

17

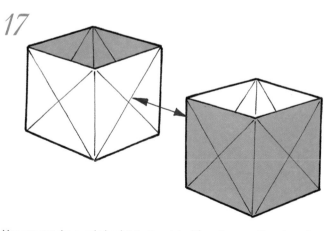

You can put the puzzle back into its original form by repeating steps 4 to 16. When the folds are softened with use, the puzzle will turn inside out much more easily.

Lucky stars

Also known as the Cinch Puzzle, because it resembles cinch blocks used to tighten tent ropes during the American Civil War, this brain teaser will have people scratching their heads. The object is to remove the stars without damaging any parts of the puzzle. The solution is surprisingly simple – once you've figured it out!

Making your lucky stars

Use two strips of paper 2 x 30 cm (¾ x 11¾ in) and a rectangle of thin craft card 7.5 x 18 cm (3 x 7 in). You will also need a needle threaded with a length of cotton, a metal ruler and craft knife.

1

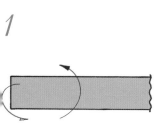

Making a star: Turn one strip of paper sideways on, coloured side on top. Make an overhand loop at the left-hand end.

2

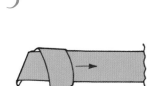

Tuck the working end through the loop already formed.

3

Pull on the end to tighten the knot. Flatten the knot into the shape of a pentagon. Adjust the short and long ends accordingly.

4

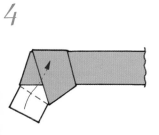

Tuck the short end inside the knot. The end should not protrude past the knot. If it does, cut or fold it a little shorter.

5

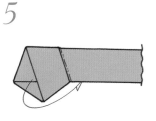

With a mountain fold, wrap one side of the knot around the long end as shown.

6

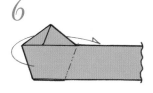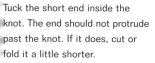

Continue wrapping the knot around the long end in a way that keeps the regular pentagon shape. As you wrap around the knot, make the folds as tight as possible.

7

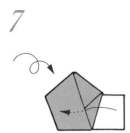

Turn the knot over. Finally, tuck the free end into the knot, making a multi-layered knot. If the end is too long, cut a little off or fold it shorter and then tuck it inside.

8

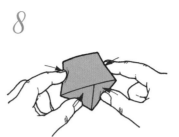

Hold the knot between two fingers of one hand at the side edges as shown. With your other hand, push gently with your thumbnail into the middle of one side, causing it to indent slightly.

9

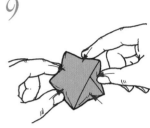

Repeat step 8 on the remaining four sides, making the knot become a three-dimensional five-pointed lucky star. Repeat steps 1 to 9 with the remaining strip of paper.

13

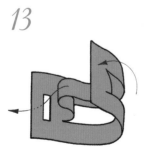

Make a loop out of the craft card between the slits and pass it through the rectangular hole.

14

Put one of the lucky stars through the loop.

15

Pull the cotton until the stars hang down evenly either side of the loop.

10

Thread the lucky stars onto a length of cotton and knot the ends to secure them as shown.

11

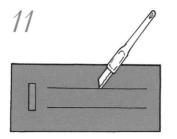

Making the puzzle: Turn the craft card sideways on and, using the metal ruler and craft knife, carefully cut two parallel slits across almost its entire length as shown. Then cut out a rectangular hole at right angles to these slits, making sure that its length is a fraction longer than the distance between the slits.

12

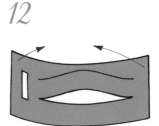

Without pressing flat, softly bend the craft card in half from side to side.

16

To complete, gently unfold the craft card, in the process flattening out the loop.

17

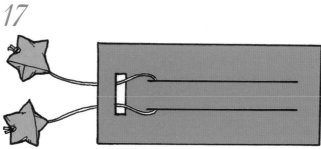

Now, ask your friends if they can remove the stars without damaging the puzzle, unfolding the stars or cutting the cotton. The solution is to repeat steps 12 and 13 and then carefully pull the stars back through the loop.

Magic wallet

Originally invented by French waiters in the 1920s as a way to store tips, this amazing creation will astound and delight. A banknote is placed behind two diagonal straps. With a quick 'Hey presto!', the note moves magically from one side of the wallet to the other, now secured behind two horizontal straps. The wallet is closed again, more magic words are spoken, and the note reappears in its original position. How is this possible?

Making your magic wallet

Use two pieces of A4 or letter paper, white side up. You will also need a pencil, ruler, pair of scissors and glue stick. Once you are familiar with the folding procedure for making the wallet's panels and hinges, you can then alter its dimensions to fit any size of banknote.

1

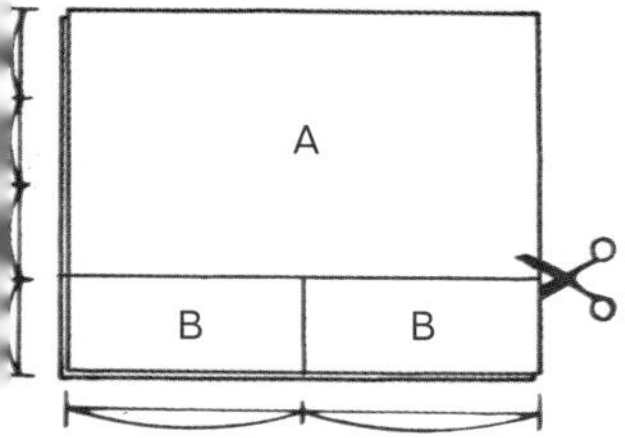

Making the wallet's panels: Turn both pieces of paper sideways on and neatly place one on top of the other. Carefully cut out rectangles A and B to the sizes shown.

2

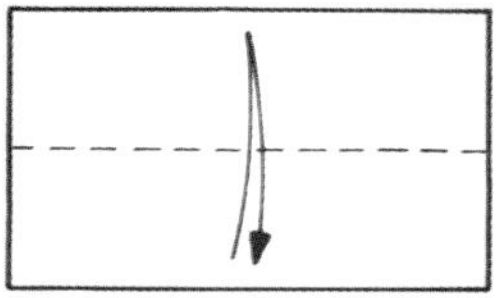

Turn one rectangle A sideways on, white side up. Fold and unfold it in half from bottom to top.

3

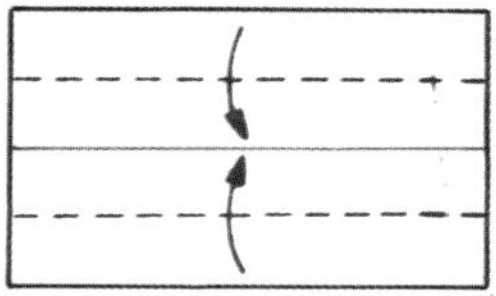

Valley fold the top and bottom edges into the middle.

4

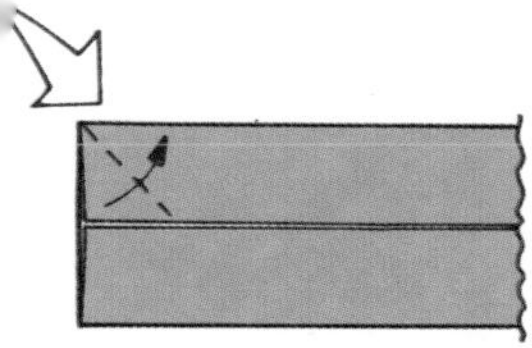

Valley fold the upper left-hand middle corner up to meet the top edge, making a triangle.

5

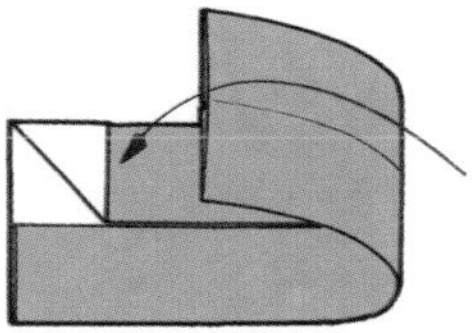

Valley fold the right-hand side over to meet the triangle's vertical edge.

6

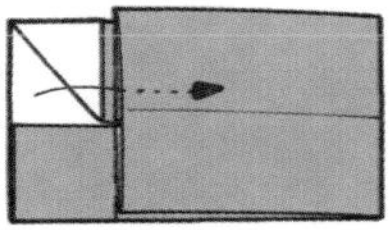

Insert the left-hand side into the adjacent pocket as shown, making a panel.

7

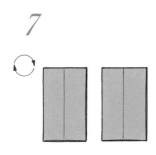

Turn the panel lengthways on. Repeat steps 2 to 7 with the remaining rectangle A.

8

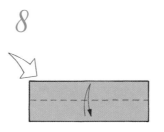

Making the wallet's straps: Turn one rectangle B sideways on, coloured side up. Fold and unfold it in half from bottom to top.

9

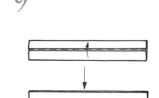

Valley fold the top and bottom edges into the middle, and then valley fold in half from bottom to top, making a strap. Repeat steps 8 and 9 with the remaining three rectangles B.

13

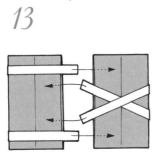

Joining the panels together: Place the panels together and carefully insert the ends of their straps into each as shown. Glue them down, completing the wallet.

14

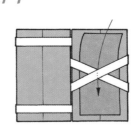

Slide a folded banknote or similar-sized rectangle of paper underneath the X-shaped straps.

15

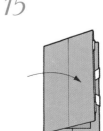

Because of its unique strap configuration, the wallet can be folded open in two directions. Close the wallet to the right.

Glue two straps together in the form of a slightly squashed X as shown.

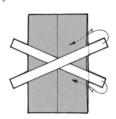

Place the X centrally on top of one panel. With a mountain fold, insert the right-hand ends of the X into the panel and glue them down.

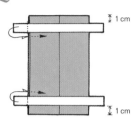

Place the remaining two straps horizontally on top of the other panel, positioning them 1 cm (⅜ in) away from the panel's top and bottom edges, with their ends protruding evenly. With a mountain fold, insert the left-hand ends of straps into the panel and glue them down.

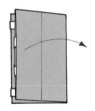

Open out the wallet from the left-hand side and …

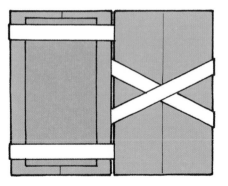

… the banknote is now held between the two horizontal straps. Again, close the wallet to the right. Once again, open it out from the left-hand side and the banknote is back underneath the X-shaped straps. Now that's magic!

1 cm

1 cm

10

11

12

16

17

Zig-Zag alien

Watch an alien appear and disappear before your very eyes, in this flexagon tribute to British magician and origami devotee Robert Harbin (1909–1978), creator of the famous 'Zig-Zag Girl' illusion. A development of 'sawing a woman in half', Harbin's trick involved dividing his assistant into three and removing the middle section of the cabinet. An impossible feat – surely?

Making your zig-zag alien

Use a piece of A4 or letter paper, white side up. You will also need a felt-tip pen, pair of scissors and roll of clear sticky tape.

1

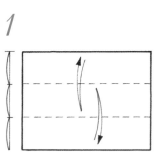

Turn the paper sideways on. Divide it horizontally into three equal sections by valley folding, then open up again.

2

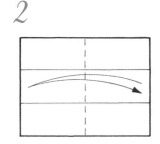

Fold and unfold in half from side to side.

3

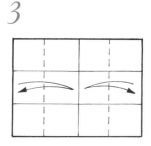

Valley fold the sides into the middle. Press flat and unfold them.

4

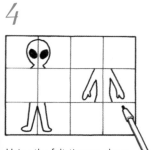

Using the felt-tip pen, draw the figure of an alien on the paper, divided up into three parts as shown.

5

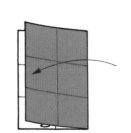

Valley fold in half from right to left.

6

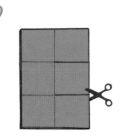

From the right-hand folded side, and through both layers of paper, carefully cut along the two horizontal fold-lines, stopping at the point where they intersect with the vertical fold-line.

7

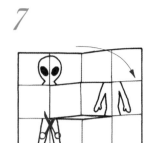

Open out the paper from left to right. Neatly cut along the middle third of the left-hand vertical fold-line, making a rectangular flap in the paper's middle.

8

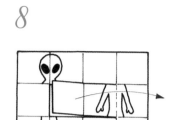

Valley fold the flap over to the right.

9

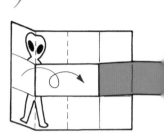

Valley fold the left-hand side into the middle and then over along ...

13

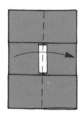

The mystery is how to find your alien in one whole piece. Valley fold the book in half from left to right.

14

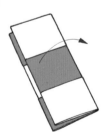

Separate the two layers at the left.

15

Mountain fold the book in half from right to left.

10

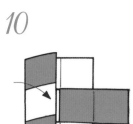

... the middle fold-line, covering up the alien.

11

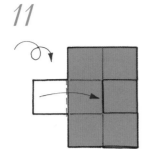

Turn the paper over. Valley fold the protruding flap over to the right and ...

12

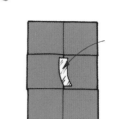

... fasten it down to the adjacent middle edge with sticky tape, making a small 'book'.

16

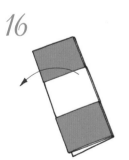

Separate the two layers at the right and ...

17

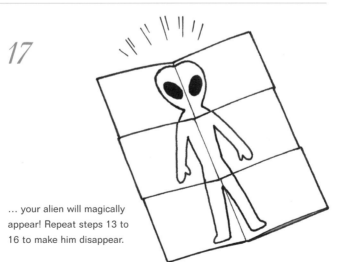

... your alien will magically appear! Repeat steps 13 to 16 to make him disappear.

Rabbit

The white rabbit has become almost synonymous with stage magicians and, along with the top hat, is commonly used as an icon to represent magic. Use your rabbit together with the magic tubes (see page 61) to produce your rabbit from 'thin air' and amaze your audience!

Making your rabbit

To make a rabbit that will sit comfortably inside the magic tubes (see page 61), use a 15 cm (6 in) square piece of paper, ideally white on one side and pink on the other. Once you have folded the rabbit, slight variations can be introduced to change its overall shape and form.

1

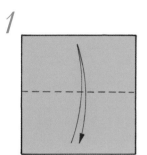

Fold and unfold the square in half from bottom to top, with the pink side on top.

2

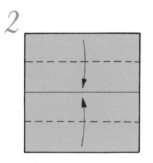

Valley fold the top and bottom edges into the middle.

3

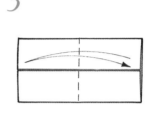

Fold and unfold in half from side to side.

4

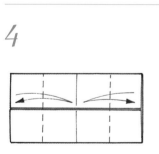

Valley fold the sides into the middle. Press flat and unfold them.

5

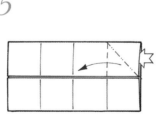

Along the adjacent vertical fold-line, pull one corner's top layer of paper over towards the middle. Press ...

6

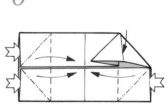

... it down neatly into the shape of a triangular point. Repeat steps 5 and 6 with the remaining three corners, making a pig base.

7

Mountain fold the left-hand point behind into the middle, at the same time letting the adjoining triangular points flick over to the left.

8

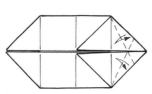

Fold and unfold the right-hand point's sloping edges over to meet the adjacent vertical fold-line.

9

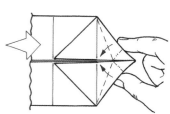

Along the fold-lines made in step 8, pinch together the right-hand point's sloping edges, making the small triangular flap that appears stand upright. This is the rabbit's tail.

13

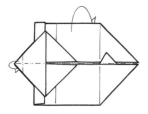

Blunt the left-hand point with a mountain fold, making the rabbit's nose. Mountain fold the paper in half from top to bottom.

14

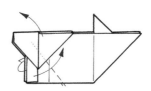

Carefully pull the left-hand points upwards, into the position shown in step 15. To complete, press the paper flat, making the rabbit's head and ears.

15

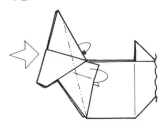

Shape the rabbit's neck and ears with a mountain fold. Repeat behind.

10

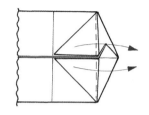

Valley fold the right-hand triangular points over along the adjacent vertical fold-line, so …

11

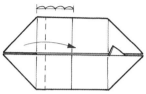

… that they lie either side of the tail. Valley fold the two left-hand points over to the right as far as shown.

12

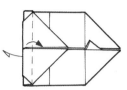

Valley fold the left-hand side over to the right along the adjacent vertical fold-line, at the same time letting the point flick up from underneath.

16

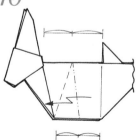

In preparation for a step fold, valley and mountain fold the middle section of paper as shown.

17

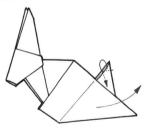

Blunt the rabbit's tail with an inside reverse fold. Unfold the valley and mountain folds made in step 16.

18

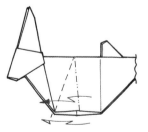

Along the fold-lines made in step 16, step fold the middle section of paper on either side.

19

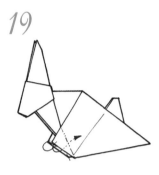

Blunt the step fold with an inside reverse fold. Repeat behind.

20

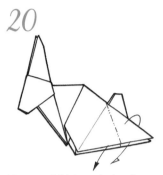

Mountain fold the right-hand point downwards slightly, making a back foot. Repeat behind.

21

Shape the back foot with an inside reverse fold as shown. Repeat behind.

22

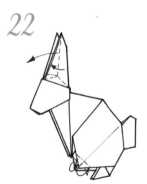

Shape the rabbit's leg with a mountain fold. Pinch an ear's sloping edges together, while at the same time flattening them down into the position shown in step 23. Repeat both procedures behind.

23

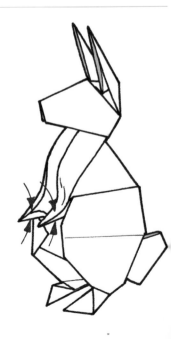

To finish, pinch the rabbit's front feet into shape as shown. Now turn to the following pages (see opposite) to make the magic tubes to complete the trick and make your rabbit magically appear!

Magic tubes

An empty red tube is shown to the
audience. Next, a blue tube is displayed
– also empty. The two tubes are nested
together and, with a magical flourish,
the performer lifts them up to reveal
an origami rabbit. This illusion provides
an effective finale to any origami magic
show, but do practise the secret moves
until they become almost automatic, to
ensure the audience won't sense that
a tricky manoeuvre is taking place.

Making your magic tubes

𝒰se four pieces of A4 or letter paper (two red for the outer tube and two blue for the inner), the same colour on both sides. You'll also need a pair of scissors. Keep your folding as accurate as possible.

1

Making the outer tube: Turn the two red pieces of paper sideways on and place one on top of the other. Fold and unfold in half from side to side. Cut along the middle fold-line, making four rectangles.

2

Take one of the rectangles created in step 1 and turn it lengthways on. Fold and unfold it in half from bottom to top.

3

Valley fold the top and bottom edges over a little to make two bands of paper that are equal in width.

7

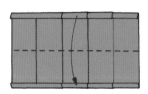

Treating them as if they were one item, carefully valley fold the joined units in half from top to bottom.

8

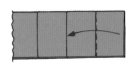

Valley fold the right-hand side in to meet the adjacent vertical edge, making a flap.

9

Valley fold the left-hand side in to meet the adjacent vertical edge. Press flat and unfold it.

4

Fold and unfold in half from side to side, so completing one unit. Repeat steps 2 to 4 with the remaining three rectangles of paper.

5

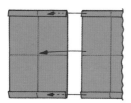

Assembling the units: From the right-hand side, insert one unit underneath the bands of paper of another, at the same time making sure that it meets the other unit's middle point as shown.

6

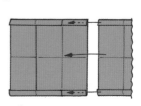

Repeat step 5 with the remaining two units.

10

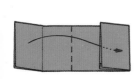

Working from the left, valley fold the left-hand side over along the second vertical edge, at the same time ...

11

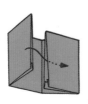

... inserting it deep into the right-hand flap, while making sure ...

12

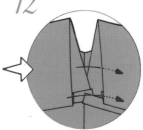

... that its bottom edges are inserted underneath the flap's bands of paper as shown.

13

Gently push the units together, making a flattened tube. Carefully open out the tube, making it become three-dimensional.

14

Pinch the tube's sides together, so making it firm and strong. This completes the outer tube.

15

Making the inner tube: Turn the two blue pieces of paper sideways on and neatly place one on top of the other. Carefully cut off from each (and discard) a strip of paper the width of which is an eighth of the rectangle's length as shown.

19

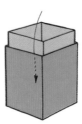

... gently place it back inside the outer tube and over the rabbit.

20

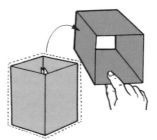

Now pick up the outer tube, again showing the audience that it is empty, and place it to one side of the inner tube.

21

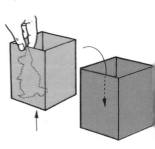

Pick up the inner tube and rabbit as if they were one item and gently place them back inside the outer tube.

16

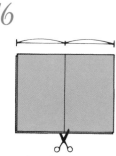

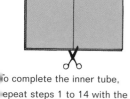

To complete the inner tube, repeat steps 1 to 14 with the rectangles of paper.

17

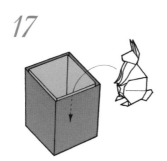

Performance: Before you perform this trick a little secret preparation has to be accomplished. Place the inner tube inside the outer tube and an origami rabbit (see page 57) inside both, as shown.

18

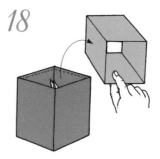

Carefully pick up the inner tube (leaving the rabbit behind), show the audience that it is empty and ...

22

Make a magical gesture, such as waving a magic wand or snapping your fingers over the tubes, and ...

23

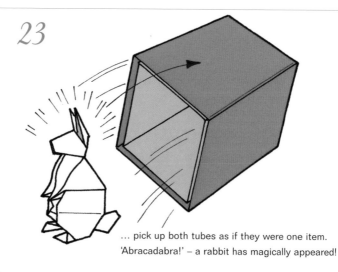

... pick up both tubes as if they were one item. 'Abracadabra!' – a rabbit has magically appeared!

Circular designs

As a story of the days of old sailing ships is told, the performer tears a square of paper to make an anchor, then an old-fashioned ship's steering wheel and, finally, the ship's crew – all from a single sheet!

Making your circular designs

Use a 36 cm (14¼ in) square piece of newspaper or coloured tissue paper. You will also need a pair of scissors. Initially, the folded papers should be marked with pencilled outlines, as shown here, to serve as a guide during the cutting and tearing. As your paper-tearing skills progress, you can omit them.

1
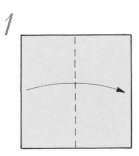
Valley fold the square in half from left to right.

2
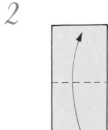
Valley fold in half from bottom to top.

3
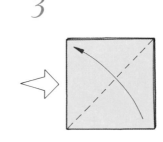
Valley fold in half from bottom right to top left, making ...

4
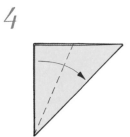
... a triangle. From the triangle's bottom point, valley fold the left-hand side over ...

5

... to lie along the opposite sloping side. Press the paper flat.

6

Carefully cut out the illustrated anchor design and discard the shaded parts as shown.

7

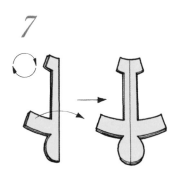

Turn the paper around, so the round knob is at the bottom. Unfold the paper once and press the middle fold-line flat to make the anchor.

8

Completely unfold the anchor to make an old-fashioned ship's steering wheel. Along the existing fold-lines ...

9

... refold the wheel back to the anchor and turn it around to look like a human figure. Cut along the middle fold-line slightly, so suggesting legs.

10

Completely unfold the paper. Break the linked figures at one point by cutting through an arm and foot as shown.

11

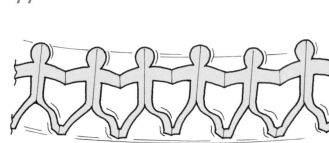

Finally, gently stretch out the paper and you will have a row of figures which represents the ship's crew!

Roll effects

Try your hand at making trees, ladders
and chains using paper-tearing effects
that involve rolling paper into a tube
rather than folding it. These traditional
techniques have delighted audiences for
years – and continue to do so to this day.

Making your tree, ladder or chain

For each trick, use two sheets of newspaper (full double-page spreads) or two rectangles of coloured tissue paper, A3 or ledger in size. You will also need a pair of scissors, glue stick and roll of clear sticky tape. If you find it hard tearing the paper with your fingers, use scissors to cut out the designs.

1

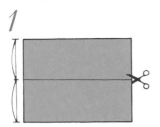

Tree: Turn the two rectangles of paper sideways on and place one on top of the other. Fold and unfold in half from bottom to top. Cut along the middle fold-line, making four rectangles.

2

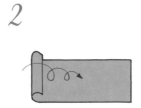

Take one of the rectangles created in step 1 and turn it sideways on. From its left-hand side loosely roll it into a tube, but before you reach the end …

3

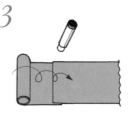

… glue on another rectangle. Keep on rolling and gluing until all the rectangles have been used up.

7

Hold the top inside centre layer and start to pull out the centre layers of paper, making sure you are holding the bottom of the tube tightly as you do so.

8

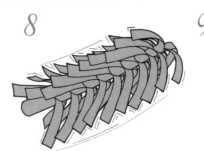

As you pull the centre layer further and further out, the tree will grow – as if by magic!

9

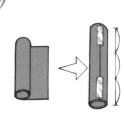

Ladder: Repeat steps 1 to 4 of the tree, but this time fastening about a third of the edge at each end of the tube with sticky tape.

4

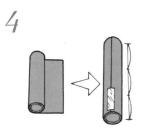

You should now have a paper tube that is approximately 4 cm (1½ in) in diameter. To prevent the tube from unrolling, fasten the bottom edge, about a third of the way up, with sticky tape.

5

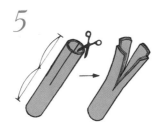

From the top of the tube carefully make four vertical cuts, cutting through all the layers of paper, to a point about midway down the tube.

6

Bend the cut pieces downwards, so that the tube resembles a peeled banana with its skin hanging down on all four sides.

10

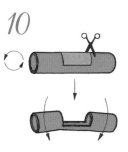

Turn the tube sideways on. Remove the middle by cutting through all the layers of paper as shown. Next, bend down the ends, making a sort of inverted U-shape.

11

Insert your forefingers into the centre of each end to begin pulling the centres upwards. This can be tricky – a sharp shake downwards will help the ladder extend.

12

Once the ladder has appeared it is now possible to extend it upwards by pulling the sides up carefully.

13

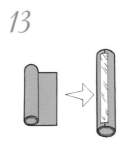

Chain: Repeat steps 1 to 4 of the tree, but now fastening the full length of the tube with sticky tape.

14

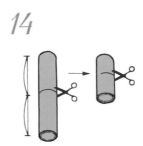

Carefully cut the tube in half. Make another cut in the middle of one of the sections, cutting most – but not all! – of the way through the tube as shown.

15

Bend the tube in half backwards, where you have cut it.

16

Hold the two tubes together. Insert your forefinger and thumb inside the tubes. Start to pull out the inside layers of paper and …

17

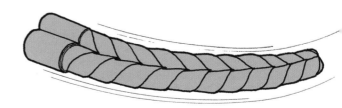

… a paper chain will grow from the inside of the cut roll. Why not make another chain with the remaining section of tube?

Möbius strip

This 'single-sided' band, named after the German
mathematician and astronomer-theorist August
Ferdinand Möbius (1790–1868), forms the basis
of this baffling trick. It's a useful trick to learn as,
in essence, it is very simple but yet makes for an
impressive stage performance if you enlist the
help of two volunteers from the audience.

Making your Möbius strip

Use a piece of A3 or ledger paper, white side up. You will also need a pair of scissors, pencil and glue stick.

1

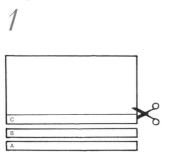

Turn the paper sideways on and carefully cut three long strips from it, each about 5 cm (2 in) wide. Label the strips, A, B and C.

2

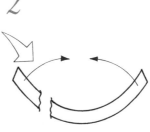

Take strip A and glue its ends together ...

3

... making a loop.

7

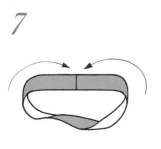

... gluing its ends together to make a loop. Now give loops B and C to members of the audience. Even though all the loops look the same ...

8

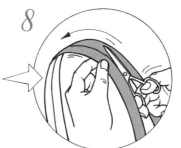

... if you carefully cut along the centre of each loop, both you and your assistants will be amazed at how different they really are.

9

Loop A will become two separate loops of paper.

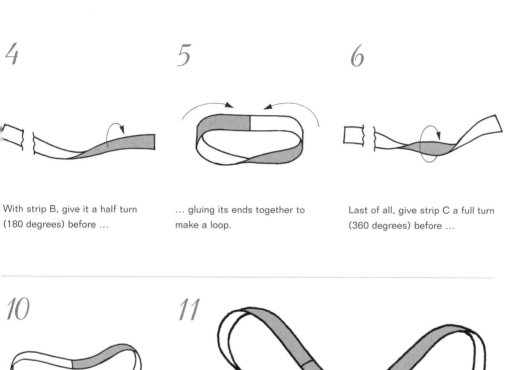

4

With strip B, give it a half turn (180 degrees) before ...

5

... gluing its ends together to make a loop.

6

Last of all, give strip C a full turn (360 degrees) before ...

10

Loop B will become a single loop that is double the size of the original loop.

11

The most baffling of all is loop C, which will become two loops linked together. Now that's paper magic for you!

Easy troublewit

Dating back to the seventeenth century, this specially pleated form of paper (also known as a 'Chinese fan' or 'fantastic fan') has long been used by performers and illusionists to entertain and amuse. Troublewit is an extremely complicated and precise piece of stage origami to make, even for professionals, so here's a simplified version which is just as effective.

Making your easy troublewit

Use two pieces of colourful but strong A3 or ledger paper. You will also need a glue stick.

1

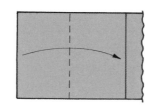

Turn the two pieces of paper sideways on and neatly glue one onto the edge of the other, as shown.

2

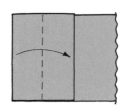

When the glue is dry, fold and unfold in half from side to side and then valley fold the left-hand side into the middle.

3

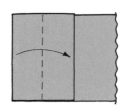

Again, valley fold the left-hand side into the middle.

4

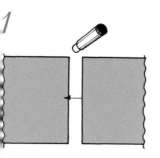

Once again, valley fold the left-hand side into the middle.

5

For the last time, valley fold the left-hand side into the middle. Press flat and unfold it.

6

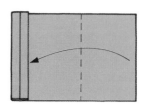

Repeat steps 2 to 5 with the right-hand side.

7

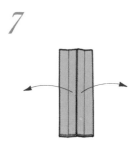

Open out the paper completely.

8

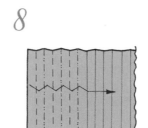

From the left-hand side, start to pleat the paper forwards and backwards along the fold-lines. In the process …

9

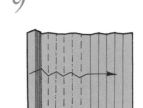

… you will have to reverse the direction of some of the fold-lines, making …

13

From the top of the troublewit, fold down slightly the pleats of each side and hold them together to make a lollipop.

14

With one hand, pinch the troublewit in its middle to make a bow-tie or butterfly.

15

With the troublewit closed, bring the top and bottom of each side together, making a rosette.

10

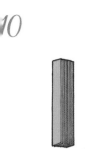

.. one folded strip of paper,
rather like a concertina. This is
a very simple version of a
professional troublewit, and here
are just a few of the many
shapes that you can make:

11

A large fan.

12

A tree.

16

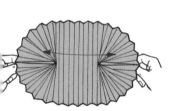

Open your hands – which are
still holding the rosette – wide,
to extend the troublewit into a
boat-like shape with rounded
ends.

17

Let one side of the boat go, and
you will have what looks like a
church window. Now, why not
try to invent a few of your own
troublewit shapes?

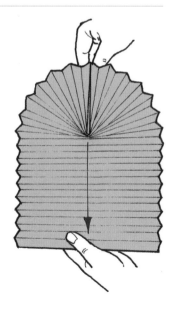

Useful addresses

The increasing popularity and international interest in origami is evident today in the number of organizations around the world that are devoted to it. Most paper-folding societies publish a newsletter or magazine containing origami-related articles and illustrations for new folds. They also hold regular meetings and yearly conventions that may include practical classes and exhibitions of the latest creations. They welcome folding enthusiasts of any age or level.

The following organizations offer a broad range of origami books, private publications on the various aspects of paper folding, packaged origami paper, and information on the many international origami associations.

British Origami Society
2a The Chestnuts, Countesthorpe
Leicestershire LE8 5TL, UK
www.britishorigami.org.uk

Origami USA
15 West 77th Street
New York, NY 10024-5192, USA
www.origami-usa.org

Visit Joseph Wu's origami website at:
www.origami.vancouver.bc.ca

Perth Origami Group (Australia)
www.origami.asn.au

Further reading

Biddle, Steve and Megumi, *Origami Inspired by Japanese Prints*. British Museum Press, in association with The Metropolitan Museum of Art, New York 1998

Eldin, Peter, *Pocket Book Of Magic*. Kingfisher Books, London 1985

Kenneway, Eric, *Complete Origami*. Ebury Press, London 1987

Slocum, Jerry and Jack Botermans, *Puzzles Old And New*. Equation, Northamptonshire 1987

Resources

You can purchase additional origami paper from Asian gift shops and toy stores, and also art and craft suppliers and stationers, some of which also stock textured and decorated paper. For beautifully patterned puzzles and tricks, try using gift wrap, or to make them even more unusual, experiment with opalescent papers or paper-backed metallic foil. All kinds of paper can be used for origami – computer paper, and even pages cut from magazines. The internet offers access to a wide choice of suppliers from all over the world.

Acknowledgements

A special thank you to Didier Boursin for sharing his Pyramid puzzle with us, and the estate of Seiryo Takekawa for the tipper; for reviewing the text, Doreen and Caroline Montgomery. Thank you to Paul and Mark Brown and John Cunliffe for testing the folding instructions. For supplying the magic wand, Davenports Magic (www.davenportsmagic.co.uk). Finally, deepest gratitude to the Eddison Sadd and Tuttle Publishing editorial and design teams.

Origami Magic project credits
Steve Biddle: Tumbler, Tangram; (introduced by): Flexi-cube, Inside-out puzzle, Magic wallet, Zig-zag alien, Magic tubes, Möbius strip, Easy troublewit
Megumi Biddle (introduced by): Lucky stars, Circular designs, Roll effects
Didier Boursin: Pyramid
Ian Carter: Rabbit
Seiryo Takekawa: Magic tipper
Traditional: Monkey climbing Mount Fuji, Flapping bird

EDDISON • SADD EDITIONS
Creative Director....Nick Eddison
Editorial Director....Ian Jackson
Managing Editor....Tessa Monina
Proofreader....Peter Kirkham
Mac Designer....Brazzle Atkins
Production....Sarah Rooney

With thanks to Steve Marwood for photography.